# Indian Vegetarian Cooking

IN A NUTSHELL

# INDIAN VEGETARIAN COOKING

## A STEP-BY-STEP GUIDE

ANNE JOHNSON

SHAFTESBURY, DORSET • BOSTON, MASSACHUSETTS • MELBOURNE, VICTORIA

First published in
Great Britain in 1999 by
ELEMENT BOOKS LIMITED
Shaftesbury, Dorset SP7 8BP

Published in the USA in 1999 by
ELEMENT BOOKS INC
160 North Washington Street,
Boston MA 02114

Published in Australia in 1999 by
ELEMENT BOOKS LIMITED
and distributed by Penguin Australia Ltd
487 Maroondah Highway, Ringwood,
Victoria 3134



NOTE FROM THE PUBLISHER
Unless specified otherwise
All recipes serve four
All eggs are medium
All herbs are fresh
All spoon measurements are level
Tablespoon = 15 ml spoon
Teaspoon = 5 ml spoon

Designed and created with Element Books by The Bridgewater Book Company Ltd.

ELEMENT BOOKS LIMITED
*Managing Editor* Miranda Spicer
*Senior Commissioning Editor* Caro Ness
*Editor* Finny Fox-Davies
*Group Production Director* Clare Armstrong
*Production Manager* Stephanie Raggett
*Production Controller* Claire Legg

THE BRIDGEWATER BOOK COMPANY
*Art Director* Terry Jeavons
*Design and page layout* Axis Design
*Project Editor* Caroline Earle
*Editor* Jo Wells
*Photography* David Jordan
*Home Economy and Styling* Judy Williams
*Picture Research* Caroline Thomas

*Printed and bound in Portugal* by
Printer Portuguesa

Library of Congress Cataloging in
Publication data available

ISBN 1 86204 480 5

*The publishers wish to thank the following for the use of pictures:*
Images Colour Library pp. 6, 8
Tony Stone Images p.7T
Science Photo Library p. 21B

# Contents

# Indian vegetarian cooking

VEGETARIANISM HAS BEEN *practiced in India for over 4,000 years. Indians prepare an enormous and varied range of vegetarian dishes, from subtle and fragrant to hot and spicy.*

On the whole nowadays people in Western societies eat less meat, if any. However, vegetarianism is not a new idea; quite the opposite, in fact, it has existed for thousands of years.

Religion is one of the reasons why vegetarianism is of such importance in India. Hinduism, which is the dominant religion, forbids meat eating. Many Hindus believe in reincarnation and consider that any animal on their plate might well contain the soul of a human being waiting to be reborn.

The other reasons are of a more practical nature. The tropical climate in most of India causes meat to deteriorate far more quickly than vegetables and in a traditionally agricultural nation, a vegetable crop allows rural self-sufficiency.

LEFT ***One of the many Hindu deities—the goddess Saravati. Hindus believe in "right living" to achieve spiritual development and follow a vegetarian diet as part of their creed.***

ABOVE *Women working in the rice fields of Goa, India.*

It is generally considered that vegetarians are likely to be healthier and to live longer than meat eaters. There are several probable reasons: vegetarians are often slimmer and eat less fat, they tend to have lower levels of blood cholesterol and therefore of heart disease; they eat more fiber and complex carbohydrates, reducing constipation and the likelihood of developing gallstones or diverticular disease.

Vegetarians are also thought to be less likely to develop some types of cancer at an early age than meat eaters. This may be because more plant foods are eaten, rather than because they do not eat meat.

Some sceptics have suggested that it is difficult to obtain enough protein from a vegetarian diet, but nutritionists generally believe that if combinations of cereals, potatoes, pulses, dairy foods, soy products, and nuts are eaten, there will be enough good quality protein in the diet.

RIGHT *Vegetable curry and rice.*

# Healthy eating

FOLLOWING A HEALTHY *diet does not mean that you have to give up all of your favorite foods. Even minor changes in eating habits can bring about major changes in health.*

If one word can be used to sum up a healthy diet, it is probably "balance:" a little of everything, and not too much of anything. Carrots are good for you, but if nothing but carrots were eaten, illness would soon follow. The simplest way of ensuring a good nutritional spread is to eat a wide and varied range of food every day from five separate food categories: cereals, bread, and other grain products; fruit; vegetables; meat, fish, eggs and pulses; and dairy produce.

BELOW ***Eating a wide variety of foods is the key to good health.***

## PROTEIN

Protein should provide around 15 per cent of the daily food intake. There are many sources of vegetable protein, such as bread, potatoes, pasta, pulses, and brown rice, but if eaten alone, the protein is nutritionally "second class." However, if different sources are combined, or eaten with dairy products, the protein becomes "first class" – equivalent to that found in meat. Soy products are an exception; they have "first class" protein.

SOYBEANS

## FATS

Fats should account for a maximum of 30 per cent of the daily calories. There are two types of fat: saturated, which are found in animal and dairy products, and unsaturated, present in most vegetable fats and fish oils. Saturated fats increase blood cholesterol and the risk of heart disease, but unsaturated fats may help protect the heart.

SESAME SEED OIL

## CARBOHYDRATES

Carbohydrates should provide half of the day's calories. They are classed either as "simple," such as sucrose (table sugar) and lactose (milk sugar), or "complex," those which are found in plant foods such as fruit and vegetables, and wholegrain cereals. The complex carbohydrates have a higher nutritional value.

NEW POTATOES

## FIBER

Although fiber has no nutritional value, it is essential for a healthy body. It promotes the passage of waste products through the intestines and, in turn, the absorption of nutrients into the bloodstream.

To maintain a healthy bowel, an average adult should eat ⅔ ounce of fiber a day. Fiber-rich foods include fresh and dried fruit and vegetables, and wholegrain cereals such as bread, rice and pasta.

FIBER-RICH CEREAL

# Sources of nutrients

INDIAN COOKS USE A WIDE VARIETY OF INGREDIENTS *and those used in Indian vegetarian cooking are mostly low in fat and calories and are particularly valuable as sources of fiber.*

## ONIONS

Onions have long been used as a cure-all. They provide a range of the B vitamins, as well as potassium, and the medicinal value has been recognized throughout history. Low in calories and fat, onions are thought to help lower blood cholesterol levels and to reduce high blood pressure. They also contain a substance which helps to prevent the blood from clotting.

ONION

## GARLIC

The sulfur compounds which give garlic its pungent odor are also the source of many of its famed health-giving properties. Garlic has antiviral and antibacterial properties and is also thought to help lower blood pressure and the level of blood cholesterol, as well as helping to prevent blood clotting, although large amounts must be eaten before there is any noticeable effect. Garlic has been used by herbalists and naturopaths as a remedy for many complaints, including asthma, arthritis, nasal congestion, and other symptoms of a cold.

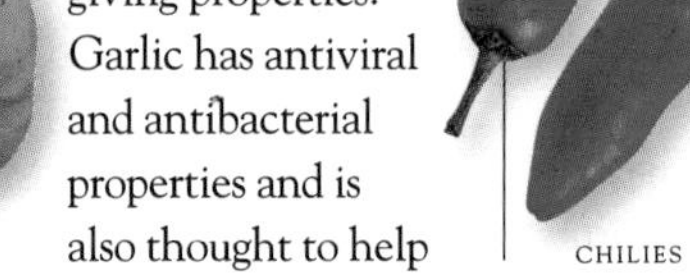

GARLIC CLOVES

## CHILIES

Chilies are a rich source of vitamin C (even richer than citrus fruits, such as lemons) and also of beta-carotene. Because they are generally eaten in such small quantities, their contribution to the diet has more to do with taste than nutrition. However, some milder varieties can be eaten in larger quantities.

CHILIES

POTATOES

## POTATOES

Potatoes supply plenty of complex carbohydrate and fiber, and some protein. Owing to the quantities that are eaten, potatoes can also be a useful source of vitamin C.

## EGGPLANTS

When cooked without oil or fat, eggplants are very low in both calories and fat and high in fiber. However, they tend to soak up large quantities of fat when they are fried. Eggplants are a source of vitamin K, which is essential for maintaining healthy blood.

EGGPLANT

## OKRA

Okra, which is also known as ladies' fingers, is high in vitamin C, calcium, phosphorus, and iron. In addition, this vegetable is a very rich source of soluble fiber, which can help to lower the levels of blood cholesterol in the body.

OKRA

## SPINACH

SPINACH

Spinach is an excellent source of the nutrient beta-carotene (the plant form of vitamin A), vitamins B6 and C, potassium, magnesium, and folate. The oxalic acid content of spinach reduces the absorption of calcium and iron, but the beneficial qualities compensate for this disadvantage. Although spinach does contain some iron, it is not such an exceptionally rich source, as was once widely believed.

## CAULIFLOWER

Cauliflower is a good source of vitamin C, folate, and potassium and it is also believed to contain sulfurous compounds that may help prevent some forms of cancer–particularly cancer of the colon.

CAULIFLOWER

## PEAS

PEAS

Peas are a useful source of a wide range of nutrients, including vitamins. They are a good source of B1 (thiamin) and vitamin C, and also contain protein, fiber, folate, and phosphorus. Canned peas lose much of their vitamin C content during canning and the blanching process reduces the vitamin C content of frozen peas. Snow peas and sugar snap peas are a good source of fiber because the pod is also eaten.

## TOMATOES

Tomatoes are a good source of vitamins C and E. They are also rich in potassium and beta-carotene and the anti-oxidant lycopene, which is valuable in helping prevent heart disease. Lycopene and the pigment that gives tomatoes their red color may help to reduce the risk of cancer.

TOMATOES

## ZUCCHINI

Zucchini are low in calories and fat, and a good source of beta-carotene, vitamin C, and folate. Most of the nutrients are located in the skin.

ZUCCHINI

## MUSHROOMS

Mushrooms are high in protein and fiber and a good source of potassium, folate, and vitamin B2, as well as a range of trace elements. They are low in calories, but they soak up a lot of fat if they are fried.

MUSHROOMS

## CUCUMBER

Cucumber has an exceptionally high water content (about 96 per cent). This means that it is low in calories and fat, and is very refreshing. It also acts as a natural diuretic and there is some evidence that the phytochemicals in cucumber can help lower blood cholesterol.

CUCUMBER

## NUTS

Nuts, such as pistachios, almonds, and cashews, are often used in Indian food. They are high in protein and unsaturated fat and they are also an excellent source of vitamins E and B. However, this is destroyed when the nuts are roasted. Pistachios, almonds, and cashews, in particular, supply significant amounts of iron, magnesium, and zinc, as well as a range of other minerals.

CASHEW NUTS

## RICE

Rice provides protein and potassium and is a valuable source of vitamin B1.

RICE

Brown rice has a higher nutritional value because the refining process to produce white rice loses much of the vitamins and minerals. A complex carbohydrate, rice is a valuable staple food, although diets based too heavily on rice can cause nutritional deficiencies, particularly in children.

Because the starch in rice is digested slowly, it provides a steady release of glucose into the blood, which is helpful for controlling blood sugar levels.

## YOGURT

Yogurt is a good source of protein and the minerals calcium and phosphorous. It also provides a good range of the B vitamins. Live yogurt contains beneficial bacteria which are necessary to maintain a healthy digestive system.

YOGURT

## PULSES AND LENTILS

High in protein, soluble fiber, low fat, and a complex carbohydrate, pulses and lentils are an invaluable source of nutrition in the vegetarian diet. They are also a good source of vitamins and minerals, including iron, folate, and potassium.

GARBANZO BEANS

# Preparing vegetables

TO BENEFIT FULLY *from the vitamins and minerals in vegetables, choose produce that is fresh and bright, has a good color, and is dry and firm with no soft patches, wrinkles, or blemishes.*

## OKRA

Wash and trim the stalks and use whole or cut as required. Okra can cause irritation, so take care when handling and wash your hands afterward.

PREPARING OKRA

## BELL PEPPERS

Cut in half lengthwise and discard the stalk, core, and seeds. To skin bell peppers, place cut side down on the broiler rack and heat under a hot broiler for about 10 minutes, or until the skin is charred and blistered. Leave until cool enough to handle, then peel away the skins.

## CHILIES

The seeds are the hottest part of a chili, so remove them for a milder dish; discard the cap, split the chili with a small, sharp knife, and scrape out the seeds. Take care when handling chilies and wash your hands after preparing them.

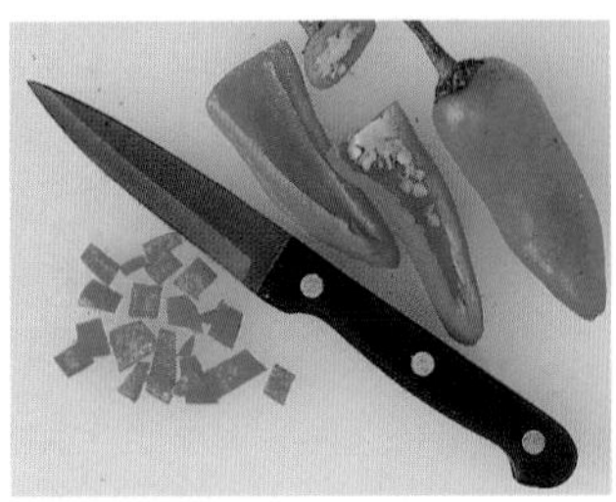

PREPARING CHILIES

## ONIONS

Slice the top off, but leave the root. For rings, remove the skin, then use a large sharp knife to cut across the width of the onion. For chopped onion, halve lengthwise through the root, then remove the skin. Put one half, cut side down and make parallel cuts, almost to the root, at right angles to it. Then cut at right angles to the first cuts.

PREPARING ONIONS

## GARLIC

Avoid cloves with green shoots, but if you must use sprouted cloves, halve lengthwise and remove the shoot.

To crush garlic, lay a clove on a chopping board and press down firmly with the flat of a large knife. Remove the skin and chop if required. Roughly chopped garlic can be made into a paste by sprinkling with a pinch of salt and mashing with the tip of a round-bladed knife.

## EGGPLANTS

To extract bitter juices, put diced, sliced, or halved eggplant in a colander. Sprinkle liberally with salt and leave to stand for 15–30 minutes. Rinse under cold running water and pat dry.

## TOMATOES

To seed, cut in half, discard the core, and remove the seeds with a teaspoon. To peel, cut a small cross in the base using a sharp knife. Place in a bowl and cover with boiling water for 20–30 seconds. Remove and plunge into cold water. The skins should then slide off easily.

PREPARING TOMATOES

## SPINACH

Choose bright or dark green spinach with no discolored or wilted leaves. Remove tough ribs, stalks, and large leaves. Wash gently, but thoroughly, in several changes of cold water to remove any dirt. Shake dry; spinach can be cooked in just the water clinging to the leaves.

# Spices

SPICES ARE *the dried aromatic parts of plants which are the leaves, seeds, roots, and bark. Their fragrant aromas have long been prized, and are a distinctive part of Indian cookery. Spices are still used for their culinary and medicinal properties. Many Indian dishes are spicy rather than hot, owing to the age-old Indian skill of blending many different spices.*

## CORIANDER SEEDS

Coriander seeds have a fragrant lemon flavor and can be used whole, ground or roasted.

CORIANDER SEEDS

## CARDAMOM

Cardamom, also known as the seed of paradise, is a highly aromatic spice. The pods can be used whole or the seeds can be removed and ground.

CARDAMOM PODS

## CHILIES

Chilies are the only really hot spice that is used in Indian cooking. A cold dairy food, such as yogurt or milk, will help to relieve the burning sensation after eating chilies.

## TURMERIC

Turmeric has a mild bitter-sweet flavor. It also imparts a strong yellow color to food.

TURMERIC

## CUMIN SEEDS

Cumin seeds are strongly aromatic and slightly bitter.

CUMIN SEEDS

## GARAM MASALA

Garam masala is a ready-made mixture of spices, providing a sweet, mild seasoning. The exact combination varies from one region to another, but, generally, garam masala consists of cardamom, cinnamon, cloves, cumin, coriander, and black peppercorns.

GARAM MASALA

## CINNAMON

Cinnamon is the bark of a tropical Asian tree. It has a strong, sweet aroma and is used to flavor a wide variety of both sweet and savory dishes.

CINNAMON STICKS

## MUSTARD SEEDS

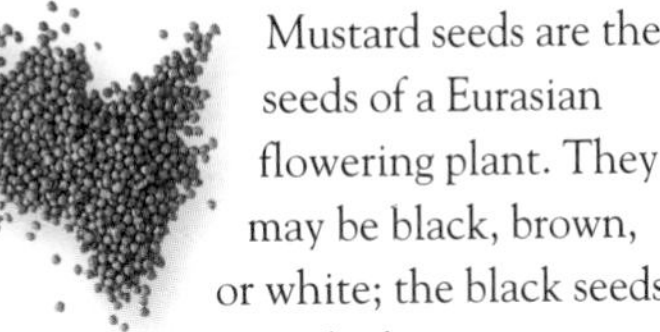

Mustard seeds are the seeds of a Eurasian flowering plant. They may be black, brown, or white; the black seeds are the hottest.

MUSTARD SEEDS

## CLOVES

Cloves are the dried, unopened buds of a tropical evergreen tree. They can be used whole or ground and impart a pungent, sharp aroma.

CLOVES

## GINGER

Ginger is cultivated through the tropics for its underground stem. It can be used fresh or powdered in sweet or savory dishes. Ginger root is also candied as a sweet.

ROOT GINGER

## BLACK PEPPER

Black peppercorns are the dried, unripe berries of a woody tropical plant. They are used either whole or ground. It is the most popular spice in the world.

BLACK PEPPER

## FENUGREEK

Fenugreek seeds are really a pulse, like mung beans. Fenugreek has a slightly bitter flavor, which can be overcome by frying or toasting it and using it in moderation.

FENUGREEK

## ASAFETIDA

This bitter spice is the gum that is exuded from the rhizomes of some plants of the genus *Ferula*, that grow in India. The resin is dried and then sold in lumps or powdered form. Uncooked, ground asafetida has an unpleasant smell. However, this disappears when the spice is heated and it takes on a more pleasant onion-like fragrance.

# Storecupboard

INDIAN COOKING DOES NOT REQUIRE *many specialty ingredients and these are now readily available from larger supermarkets and Indian foodstores.*

## RICE

The rice that is most commonly used in Indian cooking is basmati rice, which has long, slim, aromatic grains and is readily available from many supermarkets in both white and brown forms. A suitable alternative when basmati rice is not available is long grain rice.

BASMATI RICE

## GHEE

Ghee is a frequently used cooking fat in India. It is a type of clarified butter with a rich nutty taste, which is made from buffaloes' or cows' milk. All the milk solids have been removed from ghee, so that it can be heated to a high temperature without any risk of burning. It is available from specialty Indian foodstores and some supermarkets and does not need to be refrigerated. Butter can be used instead of ghee or, alternatively, use a neutral-flavored vegetable oil, such as peanut oil or sunflower oil.

GHEE

## COCONUT MILK

COCONUT MILK

Coconut milk can be made with either fresh or shredded coconut. Fresh coconut will produce milk that has a richer flavor and a creamier texture. Canned coconut milk and coconut milk powder are available from many supermarkets or from specialty Indian foodstores.

## YOGURT

Yogurt in India is usually made from buffaloes' milk and it is both creamy and firm in texture. Use a firm-textured, unsweetened yogurt wherever yogurt is required for a recipe. You can make your own by using a yogurt starter from a health food store.

YOGURT

## PANIR

Panir is an Indian curd cheese that is made by curdling milk and separating off the creamy white curds. The curds are then pressed into a cheese to remove any moisture. The cheese has a delicate flavor and is cut into pieces and sautéed for use in dishes such as mattar panir and vegetable biriyani. It can be bought in packets from specialty Indian foodstores. Once the packet has been opened, the panir should be used very quickly as it does not keep well.

PANIR

## GRAM FLOUR

Gram flour or besan, is made from finely ground garbanzo beans, it is pale yellow and has a distinctive flavor. Gram flour is available from Indian foodstores.

GRAM FLOUR

## SPICES

It is always better to buy whole dried spices and grind them as required, using a small electric grinder or a pestle and mortar. The art of Indian cookery is in blending the spices and this is usually a matter of personal preference. Subtle changes can be made by increasing or decreasing the quantities given in a recipe, according to taste.

## PULSES AND LENTILS

These are essential storecupboard items. Dried pulses and lentils keep very well, but they are best stored in an airtight container and used within six months of purchase. Canned garbanzo beans are also available.

GARBANZO BEANS

# Regional variations

INDIA IS *a vast country about the size of Europe, and is separated from the rest of Asia by the Himalayas. Over the centuries, India has been home to a number of different nationalities, so it is not surprising that it has been influenced by several different cuisines, including Portuguese, English, and Persian.*

Indian cookery should not be thought of as only one type of food, but instead as a collection of individual regional styles. As a general rule, the food tends to get hotter and spicier the further south you go.

## EASTERN INDIA

The main cooking fat used in the east, which comprises Bengal and Bihar, is mustard oil, which is made from the lush mustard plants that cover the fields of the region. The oil imparts a slightly sweet taste to everything that is cooked in it. Regional spices include cloves, mustard, cumin, anise, and fenugreek and the area is famous for its fragrant sweetmeats and savory dishes.

MUSTARD OIL

## WESTERN INDIA

Western India comprises Goa and Bombay. The food is rather hot and spicy and popular ingredients include vinegar, coconut milk, and tamarind. Cooking tends to be long and slow, which gives dishes a rich, succulent flavor.

Bombay is famed for its ice creams, which are usually fruit-based, and for its long sweet drinks, called sharbats that are based on fruit and yogurt.

BOMBAY ICE-CREAM

## SOUTHERN INDIA

Southern India is dominated by Hindus. As they are vegetarians, a lot of vegetables and rice are eaten here, with coconut, coconut milk, mustard, and tamarind being the main flavoring. Chilies are used generously in this region, resulting in many hot, fiery recipes.

COCONUT

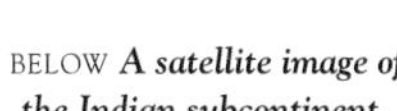

BELOW ***A satellite image of the Indian subcontinent.***

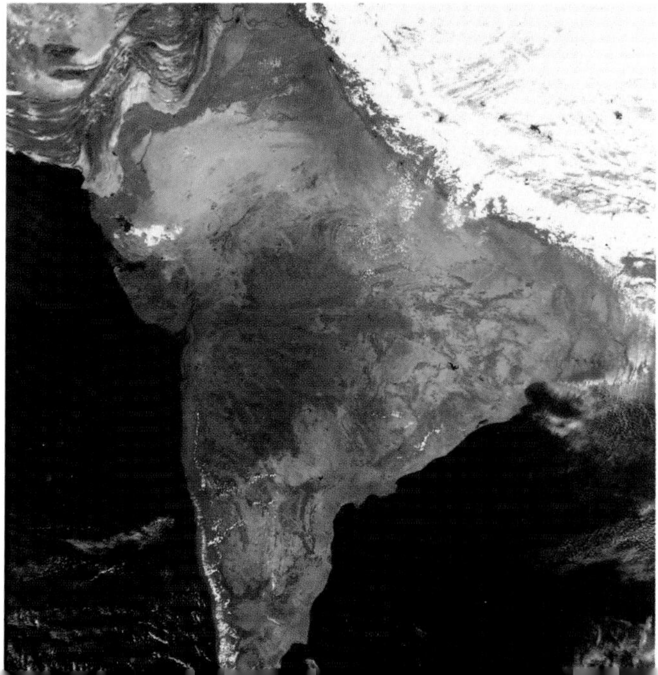

## NORTHERN INDIA

Northern India enjoys a subtle, sophisticated cuisine, dominated by the Punjabi and Kashmiri cooking styles. Wheat is more widely used rather than rice here, and ghee (clarified butter) is the preferred cooking medium.

## CENTRAL INDIA

Vegetarian food is less prevalent in the central part of India, because the Mughals, who historically dominated the region, were meat eaters.

# Mulligatawny Soup

BRITISH IN ITS INSPIRATION, *but Indian in its ingredients, mulligatawny soup literally means pepper or chili water.*

**INGREDIENTS**

*1 onion, finely chopped*

*2 garlic gloves, finely chopped*

*½-inch piece of ginger root, grated*

*1 ounce ghee*

*1 teaspoon each ground coriander, turmeric, fenugreek, and cumin*

*¼ teaspoon chili powder*

*2½ cups vegetable stock*

*1 teaspoon lemon juice*

*⅔ cup coconut milk*

*salt and black pepper*

*1–2 tablespoons cooked rice (optional)*

*lemon wedges, to serve*

GINGER ROOT

1 Gently fry the onion, garlic, and ginger in the ghee in a large saucepan until soft. Stir in all the ground spices.

2 Add the vegetable stock and cook over medium heat so the mixture comes slowly to a boil.

3 Add the lemon juice, coconut milk, and seasoning. Simmer gently, uncovered, for 5–10 minutes.

4 Stir the rice, if using, into the soup just before serving with wedges of lemon.

# Vegetable Samosas

CRISP AND SPICY, *samosas work equally well as an appetizer or a snack. They can be served hot or cold.*

**INGREDIENTS**

**FOR THE PASTRY**

*2⅔ cups all-purpose flour*

*1 teaspoon salt*

*½ cup margarine, chopped*

*scant ½ cup water*

**FOR THE FILLING**

*1 tablespoon ghee*

*pinch of ground asafetida*

*pinch of ground turmeric*

*1½ teaspoons mustard seeds*

*11 ounces parboiled potatoes, diced*

*scant ½ cup peas, cooked*

*2 small fresh green chilies, seeded and chopped*

*1 teaspoon salt*

*1 teaspoon garam masala*

*1 heaped tablespoon chopped cilantro*

*milk, for brushing*

*oil, for deep-frying*

1 Rub the margarine into the flour and salt with your fingertips until the mixture resembles fine bread crumbs. Stir in the water, cover with a damp cloth, and set aside.

GREEN CHILIES

**VARIATIONS**

- Use parboiled carrots in place of half the potatoes.
- Use water to seal the dough instead of milk.

2 Cook the asafetida powder, turmeric, mustard seeds, potatoes, peas, chilies, and salt in the ghee, over medium heat, stirring, for 2 minutes. Cover and cook gently for 10 minutes.

3 Off the heat, add the garam masala and the cilantro, stir well and leave to cool.

Divide the dough into 8 equal pieces and roll out each piece into a 6-inch round. Cut in half, using a sharp knife.

4 Work with 1 half round at a time (cover the others with a damp cloth). Brush the edges with milk and spoon 1½ teaspoons of the filling into the center. Fold in the corners, overlapping them to form a cone. Fold and seal to make a triangle. Deep-fry a few at a time, until golden. Drain on paper towels.

# Onion Bhajis

DRY AND EASY TO EAT *with the fingers, with no risk of spillage, onion bhajis are a convenient snack.*

**INGREDIENTS**

*7 tablespoons vegetable oil*
*1 teaspoon mustard seeds*
*½ teaspoon ground turmeric*
*3–4 large onions, sliced*
*1¼ cups gram flour, sifted*
*salt*
*½ teaspoon chili powder*

1 Fry the mustard seeds and turmeric in 4 tablespoons of the oil in a saucepan over medium heat until the seeds begin to pop. Add the onions and fry gently for 10 minutes until they are soft.

### VARIATIONS

- Add some sliced garlic to the onion.
- Use red onions for a slightly sweeter flavor.
- Use shallots for a slightly milder flavor.

**2** Add 1 tablespoon gram flour at a time, stirring thoroughly after each addition. Continue in this way until all the flour has been used. Add the chili powder, season with salt, and stir well again.

SLICED ONIONS

**3** Divide the mixture into 4 pieces and mold each piece into a ball. Fry quickly in the remaining oil, using a spatula to prevent the bhajis from falling apart.

GRAM FLOUR

### COOK'S TIP

Gram flour is made from garbanzo beans and is used in India to make pakoras and to thicken sauces. It is available in specialty Indian foodstores and larger supermarkets. You can make your own by finely grinding garbanzo beans.

# Potato Cakes

POTATO CAKES *are often seen for sale on street corners in India and can be eaten either as a snack or as part of a meal, accompanied by chutney or yogurt.*

**INGREDIENTS**

*1 cup yellow split peas, soaked overnight and drained*

*2½ cups salted water*

*salt*

*2 tablespoons vegetable oil, plus extra for frying*

*5 fenugreek seeds*

*1 onion, chopped*

*1 tablespoon seeded and chopped fresh green chilies*

*a pinch each of ground ginger and coriander*

*2⅔ cups cold mashed potato*

*1 egg, beaten*

1 Boil the split peas in the salted water for 15 minutes. Drain and allow to cool in a covered bowl.

**COOK'S TIP**

The potato cakes can be prepared to the point where they are fried, up to a day in advance.

2 Cook the fenugreek seeds in the oil over medium heat for 5–10 seconds, or until they begin to change color. Add the onion and fry for a further 2–3 minutes, or until it begins to brown.

3 Add the chilies, ginger, coriander, cooked split peas, and mashed potato.

4 Form into flat 3-inch round cakes. Dip into the beaten egg and fry gently in batches in hot oil for about 8–10 minutes on each side, until well browned.

**VARIATIONS**

- Use butter rather than oil to fry the cakes.
- Use green peas instead of yellow split peas.
- Add chopped cilantro with the chilies.

YELLOW SPLIT PEAS

# Mattar Panir

THIS MILD DISH *of peas cooked with Indian curd cheese, turmeric, and ginger has a subtle combination of flavors.*

**INGREDIENTS**

*10 ounces panir, cubed*
*6 tablespoons vegetable oil*
*2 onions, finely chopped*
*2 cups water*
*salt*
*1 pound peas*
*1 teaspoon sugar*
*2 teaspoons ground turmeric*
*1 teaspoons ground chilies*
*1 tablespoon grated ginger root*
*1 tablespoon chopped cilantro, to garnish*

PANIR

1 Fry the panir in the oil in a heavy-based skillet over medium heat until golden brown, turning frequently and gently and being careful not to allow it to burn or stick. Remove, drain on absorbent paper towels and set aside.

**VARIATIONS**

- Substitute spinach for peas.
- Use 1 or 2 chopped fresh chilies instead of ground chilies.

2 Add the onion and fry for 3–4 minutes, or until soft, stirring constantly.

3 Add the water and salt and bring to a boil. Stir in the peas and sugar, cover, and simmer for 10 minutes, or until the peas are almost tender and the water has evaporated. Uncover the pan for the last few minutes, if necessary.

4 Stir in the fried panir, the turmeric, chili, and ginger. Cover, lower the heat and simmer for 10 minutes. Garnish with cilantro.

# Eggplant Bharta

BROILED EGGPLANT *is delicately spiced with chilies, turmeric, and coriander, producing a delectable combination of flavors.*

**INGREDIENTS**

*1 medium eggplant*

*3 tablespoons vegetable oil*

*1 large onion, finely chopped*

*1 garlic clove, crushed*

*3 tomatoes, chopped*

*1–2 fresh green chilies, seeded and finely chopped*

*½ teaspoon ground turmeric*

*1 tablespoon ground coriander*

*1 tablespoon finely chopped cilantro, plus 1 tablespoon, to garnish*

*salt*

*2 tablespoons lemon juice*

**VARIATIONS**

- Add ½ teaspoon chili powder.
- Add 1 teaspoon finely chopped ginger root.
- Substitute a small can of chopped tomatoes for fresh tomatoes.

1 Cook the aubergine under a hot broiler for 20 minutes, or until blackened on all sides and soft, turning frequently.

2 Leave to cool, then rinse under cold running water and peel off the skin. Mash the flesh with a fork and set aside.

3 Gently fry the onion and garlic in the vegetable oil in a large, skillet, stirring constantly, for 5–6 minutes, or until the onion is soft, but not colored.

4 Add the tomatoes, chilies, and turmeric and fry for a further 2–3 minutes. Stir in the ground coriander, chopped cilantro and salt.

5 Add the eggplant flesh and sprinkle with lemon juice. Fry gently for 10 minutes, stirring occasionally. Garnish with cilantro.

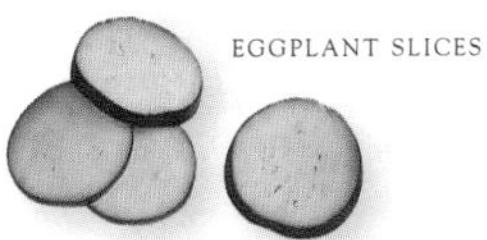
EGGPLANT SLICES

# Vegetable Curry

ESSENTIAL TO *everyone's Indian cookery repertoire, vegetable curry comes in many different versions.*

**INGREDIENTS**

*3 tablespoons vegetable oil*

*2 tablespoons fennel seeds*

*2 large onions, sliced*

*9 cardamom pods, bruised*

*1 teaspoon chili powder*

*2 tablespoons ground coriander*

*2 tablespoons cumin seeds, lightly crushed*

*1-inch piece of ginger root, grated*

*1¼ cups vegetable stock*

*salt*

*1 cup diced potatoes*

*3 medium carrots, sliced*

*1½ cups shelled peas*

*2 small eggplants, sliced*

*1¼ cups sliced zucchini*

*2 tablespoons chopped cilantro, plus extra to garnish*

*2 tablespoons unsweetened yogurt*

CARDAMOM PODS

1 Heat the oil in a large saucepan. Fry the fennel seeds for a few seconds. Add the onion and fry over medium heat until soft and golden.

2 Stir in the cardamom pods, chili powder, ground coriander, cumin, and ginger.

3 Fry for 1 minute. Add the stock, season, and add the potatoes, carrots, peas, and eggplants. Bring to a boil, cover, and simmer, stirring occasionally, for 10–15 minutes.

4 Add the zucchini and simmer, uncovered, for 15 minutes, stirring from time to time. Check that all the vegetables are cooked.

**VARIATIONS**

- Use green beans, trimmed and cut into 1-inch lengths, instead of peas.
- Add ½ cup toasted cashew nuts, roughly chopped, toward the end of cooking.

5 Stir in the chopped cilantro. Drizzle over the yogurt and garnish with chopped cilantro.

**COOK'S TIP**

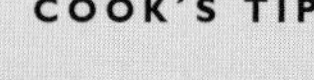

A delicious way to garnish this curry is to sprinkle it with a little finely grated fresh coconut or with some fine shredded coconut.

# Vegetable Biriyani

THIS DELICIOUS AND VERSATILE *one-pot meal is perfect for hearty appetites and makes an ideal main meal for the family.*

**INGREDIENTS**

*2 cups brown basmati rice, soaked for 20–30 minutes*

*2 large onions, finely chopped*

*2 tablespoons vegetable oil*

*1 large garlic clove, chopped*

*6 cloves*

*4 green cardamom pods*

*1 teaspoon each ground turmeric and garam masala*

*6 ounces diced vegetables, such as carrots, cauliflower, peas, and zucchini*

*salt*

*2¼ cups vegetable stock*

*2 ounces panir*

*¼ cup golden raisins*

*¾ cup chopped cashew nuts*

**COOK'S TIP**

Use white basmati rice instead of brown, but remember that it is less rich in nutrients and fiber.

1 Fry the onion in oil in a large saucepan until soft and just golden, reserve half. Add the turmeric, cardamom, garlic, cloves and garam masala. Cook for 2–3 minutes.

2 Rinse the rice in cold running water. Drain well. Stir into the pan and cook for 5 minutes, until it glistens.

3 Add the vegetables and then pour in the stock, and bring to a boil. Cover and simmer for 20–25 minutes, or until most of the liquid has been absorbed and the rice is tender.

4 Add the panir, golden raisins, and nuts. Cover and cook gently for 5 minutes, or until all the moisture has evaporated. Serve piping hot, garnished with the reserved fried onion.

# Okra Masala

LADIES' FINGERS, *or okra, is an interesting and nutritious vegetable, which lends itself perfectly to this recipe.*

INGREDIENTS

*1 heaping tablespoon ground coriander*

*1 heaping teaspoon ground cumin*

*1 teaspoon each fennel seeds, mustard seeds, fenugreek, and ground turmeric*

*2 teaspoons sesame seeds*

*pinch of chili powder*

*2 tablespoons vegetable oil*

*1 small onion, finely chopped*

*3 garlic cloves, crushed*

*scant 1 cup water*

*1 teaspoon soft brown sugar*

*2–3 tablespoons tomato paste*

*1 pound small okra*

*salt*

OKRA

1 Gently fry the spices in the oil in a heavy-based saucepan, stirring constantly, for 1 minute.

2 Add the onion and garlic and fry for 3 minutes.

3 Stir in 4–5 tablespoons of water, the sugar and tomato paste. Then cover and simmer gently for 1 minute.

**VARIATIONS**

- Use unsweetened yogurt instead of tomato paste.
- Use equal quantities of okra and green split peas instead of okra alone.
- Add 1 sliced fresh red chili toward the end of the cooking time for a little extra heat.

4 Add the okra and the remaining water, season, and stir thoroughly. Bring to a boil and simmer over low heat for about 10–12 minutes, or until the okra are tender and the curry is almost dry.

# Spinach with Tomatoes

WITH ITS DELICIOUS COMBINATION *of bright colors and fresh flavors, this dish looks as good as it tastes.*

**INGREDIENTS**

*3 tablespoons vegetable oil*

*2 onions, finely sliced*

*2 garlic cloves, crushed*

*½-inch piece of ginger root, grated*

*2 teaspoons each chili powder, garam masala, coriander seeds, ground coriander and cumin seeds*

*salt*

*1½ pounds fresh leaf spinach, washed, dried and shredded*

*6 tomatoes, roughly chopped*

FRESH LEAF SPINACH

**COOK'S TIP**

In an emergency, you can use frozen spinach instead of fresh, but the flavor and color will not be so good.

1 Fry the onions and garlic in the oil in a large, heavy-based saucepan over medium heat for about 5 minutes, or until they are soft and just turning golden.

2 Add the ginger and fry for 3–4 minutes. Stir in the spices and salt and continue frying for 1 minute.

3 Add the spinach and stir until mixed with the onions and spices.

**VARIATIONS**

- Use canned tomatoes instead of fresh ones.
- Use 1 teaspoon ground ginger if ginger root is not available.
- Use lentils instead of tomatoes.

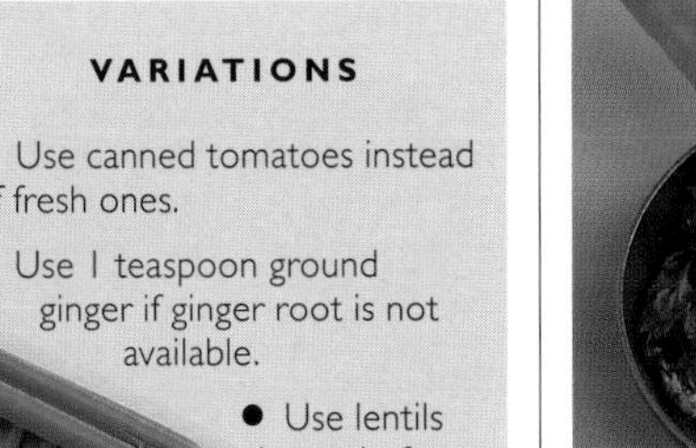

4 Stir in the tomatoes and bring to a simmer, stirring. Simmer for 10–15 minutes, adding boiling water if the mixture becomes dry and the spinach looks like sticking to the pan.

TOMATOES

# Spicy Garbanzo Beans

GARBANZO BEANS *are a robust pulse that lend themselves well to the addition of a number of spices.*

**INGREDIENTS**

*1¼ cups garbanzo beans, soaked in 3¾ cups water overnight*

*1 onion, finely sliced*

*3 tablespoons vegetable oil*

*3 garlic cloves, crushed*

*pinch of ground asafetida*

*½ teaspoon cumin seeds*

*4 cloves*

*1-inch piece of ginger root, grated*

*1–2 fresh green chilies, seeded and finely chopped*

*1 teaspoon each ground coriander and cumin*

*salt*

*2 tablespoons lemon juice*

*1 tablespoon coarsely chopped cilantro*

*lemon wedges, to garnish*

GROUND ASAFETIDA

1 Bring the garbanzo beans to a boil in the soaking water, cover and simmer for 1 hour, or until tender. Drain, reserving the cooking liquid, and set aside.

2 Gently fry the onion in the oil in a large saucepan for 6–7 minutes, until soft. Add the garlic and fry for a few more minutes. Stir in the asafetida, cumin seeds, and cloves and allow to sizzle for a few seconds.

3 Add the garbanzo beans, ginger, chilies, coriander, cumin and the salt and fry for 5 minutes. Add 1 cup reserved cooking liquid and cook for 20–25 minutes, stirring occasionally.

4 Stir in the lemon juice and sprinkle with chopped cilantro. Garnish with the lemon wedges.

CLOVES

**VARIATIONS**

- Use canned garbanzo beans instead of dried, adding water instead of the cooking liquid.
- Use finely chopped fresh green chili instead of cilantro to garnish.
- Lime wedges can be used instead of lemon, to garnish.

# Marinated Cauliflower

EVEN A BRIEF MARINATING *makes all the difference to cauliflower, which quickly soaks up the flavor.*

**INGREDIENTS**

*⅔ cup unsweetened yogurt*

*1 heaping teaspoon ground ginger*

*1 heaping tablespoon chopped cilantro*

*1 heaping teaspoon sugar*

*salt*

*1½ pounds cauliflower, broken into flowerets*

*1 onion, sliced*

*2 tablespoons vegetable oil*

*1¼ cups raisins*

*2 cups shelled peas*

*2–3 fresh red chilies, finely chopped*

*1 heaping teaspoon garam masala*

*scant ½ cup hot water*

1 Stir the yogurt, ginger, cilantro, sugar, and salt together in a large bowl. Add the cauliflower and set aside to marinate for at least 2 hours.

2 Fry the onion in the oil in a saucepan over medium heat for 5 minutes, or until soft and just golden.

3 Add the raisins, peas, cauliflower and marinade, chilies, garam masala, and hot water. Stir thoroughly until all the ingredients are well amalgamated.

4 Cover and simmer gently for about 15 minutes, or until the cauliflower is tender and the liquid has evaporated. Serve as an accompaniment or with chapatis.

RED CHILIES

**VARIATIONS**

- Substitute green chilies for the red.
- Grated ginger root can be used instead of ground ginger.
- Use broccoli flowerets instead of cauliflower.

RAISINS

# Dhal

MAKE THIS LENTIL DISH *as mild or as spicy as you like. It is a popular Indian staple and can be very filling.*

**INGREDIENTS**

*1 cup green or brown lentils*

*5 cups salted water*

*3 tablespoons vegetable oil*

*1 large onion, chopped*

*1 fresh green chili, chopped*

*½ teaspoon chili powder*

*1 teaspoon cumin seeds*

*pinch of ground asafetida*

LENTILS

**VARIATION**

- Use ground coriander instead of cumin seeds.
- Use shallots in place of the onion.

1 Bring the lentils to a boil in the salted water in a saucepan, then simmer for 1½ hours. Drain well.

2 Meanwhile, fry the onion in 1 tablespoon of the oil in another pan over medium heat for 5 minutes, or until soft and just golden. Add the chili and chili powder.

3 Stir the lentils into the onion and cook for 10 minutes.

4 Quickly fry the cumin and asafetida in the remaining oil over medium heat for 30 seconds. Pour the spicy oil over the lentils and serve.

# Fried Rice

THIS DISH *is a delicious accompaniment to curries and it is also an excellent way of using leftover rice.*

**INGREDIENTS**

*1¾ cups basmati rice, soaked for 30 minutes and drained*

*3¾ cups water*

*3 tablespoons ghee*

*2-inch cinnamon stick, broken in half*

*2 bay leaves*

*4–6 green cardamom pods*

*3 large onions, thinly sliced*

*3 fresh green chilies, finely sliced*

*salt*

CINNAMON STICKS

**VARIATIONS**

- Add 2 tablespoons golden raisins at the last minute.
- Add 1–2 tablespoons pistachios just before serving.
- Stir 2 crushed garlic cloves with the onions and chilies.

1 Bring the rice to a boil in the water, in a large saucepan. Stir, lower the heat, cover and cook for 20 minutes, or until all the water has been absorbed.

2 Fry the cinnamon, bay leaves and cardamom pods in the ghee in a large skillet over medium to high heat for a few seconds, or until all the ingredients sizzle.

3 Lower the heat, add the onions and green chilies and fry for 8–10 minutes, or until the onions are soft and just turning golden brown, stirring frequently.

4 Add the rice, season with salt, and fry for 10 minutes, or until the rice is heated through, stirring frequently. Remove and discard the cinnamon and bay leaves.

# Chapatis

CHAPATIS ARE A *low-calorie, fat-free Indian bread, although some Indian cooks do brush them with a little melted butter before serving. They are a filling accompaniment.*

**INGREDIENTS**

*½ cup all-purpose flour, plus extra for rolling*

*½ cup whole wheat flour*

*salt*

*about 5 tablespoons water*

**Makes 6**

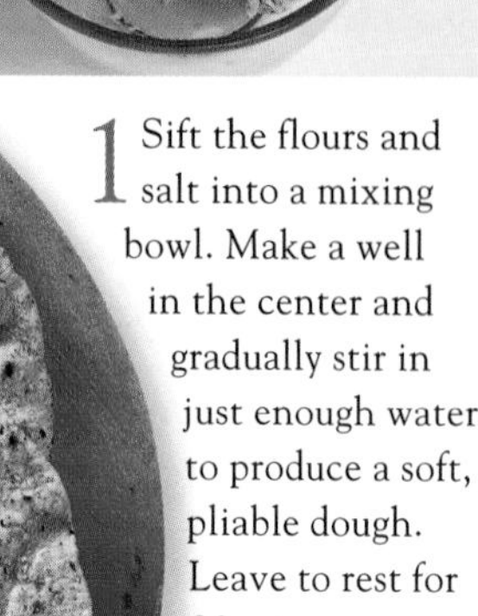

1 Sift the flours and salt into a mixing bowl. Make a well in the center and gradually stir in just enough water to produce a soft, pliable dough. Leave to rest for 30 minutes.

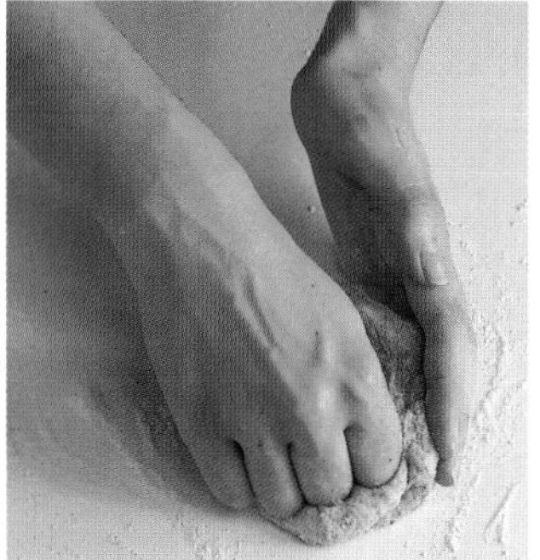

2 Knead the dough on a lightly floured surface for about 10 minutes, or until smooth and elastic.

3 Divide the dough into 6 golf-ball-size pieces and dip into all-purpose flour. On the floured surface, flatten with a rolling pin to form 6-inch pancakes.

4 Heat a cast-iron skillet until very hot, then reduce the heat to low and cook the chapatis, 1 at a time, for 1 minute on each side, or until pale brown blisters develop on both sides.

5 Eat hot, straight from the skillet or keep warm wrapped in cooking foil in the oven until ready to serve.

**VARIATIONS**

- Use whole wheat flour on its own instead of a mixture.
- Fill with chopped spinach flavored with cumin and ginger.
- Use a little ghee or vegetable oil in the skillet.

# Mango and Ginger Chutney

IF YOU CAN *master this simple recipe you will never need to buy a jar of mango chutney again.*

**INGREDIENTS**

*1¼ cups water*

*½ teaspoon ground turmeric*

*1½ pounds just ripe mangoes, peeled, pitted and sliced*

*2 fresh green chilies, seeded and finely chopped*

*½ cup soft brown sugar*

*1 teaspoon mustard seeds*

*1 teaspoon ground cumin*

*2-inch piece of ginger root, grated*

*1 heaping tablespoon golden raisins*

*1 tablespoon white wine vinegar*

**Makes 1 jar**

1 Add the turmeric to the salted water and bring it to a boil. Add the chopped mangoes and chilies and cook over medium heat for about 3–4 minutes, or until the mangoes are just cooked.

2 Add the sugar, mustard seeds, cumin, ginger, golden raisins, and vinegar and increase the heat to high. Cook for 20–25 minutes, or until soft, stirring as the chutney thickens.

3 Remove from the heat and allow to cool. Serve warm or cold. Store the chutney in the refrigerator for 3–4 days.

### COOK'S TIP

It is important to use mangoes at the right stage of ripeness. They should be firm, only just ripe, and certainly not soft.

To extend the shelf life of the chutney, pour it into hot sterilized jars and cover with an airtight lid. It will then last for several months.

### VARIATIONS

- Use dried mangoes instead of fresh ones; soak in water overnight.
- Raisins can be used instead of golden raisins.
- Add a pinch of chili powder.

# Raita

THIS SIDE DISH of yogurt and cucumber *is a cooling accompaniment to the hottest curry.*

## INGREDIENTS

*4 ounces cucumber, cut into matchsticks*

*salt*

*1¼ cups unsweetened yogurt*

*2–3 scallions, thinly sliced*

*pinch of ground cumin*

*cucumber slices or chopped cilantro or mint, to garnish*

UNSWEETENED YOGURT

### VARIATIONS

- Use a banana instead of cucumber.
- Add a fresh green chili, seeded and finely chopped.
- Add lemon or lime juice to taste.

1 Put the cucumber in a colander and sprinkle generously with salt. Leave to drain for 30 minutes. Pat dry with absorbent paper towels.

2 Meanwhile, beat the yogurt well with a fork until it is smooth and thick.

SCALLIONS

3 Stir in the cucumber, scallions and cumin.

4 Set the raita aside for 30 minutes to allow the flavor to develop, then transfer to a serving dish and chill in the refrigerator.

# Jalebi

SWEET AND STICKY, *these deep-fried batter coils are a great favorite with adults and children alike.*

**INGREDIENTS**

*1½ cups all-purpose flour*
*½ cup gram flour*
*4 tablespoons unsweetened yogurt*
*¼ ounce fresh yeast*
*1¼ cups water*
*generous 1 cup sugar*
*½ teaspoon ground saffron*
*½ teaspoon ground cardamom*
*vegetable oil, for deep-frying*

FRESH YEAST

**COOK'S TIP**

To test the syrup without a thermometer, dip 2 teaspoons into the syrup. Lift them out and quickly press the backs together. If the syrup is ready, when you pull the spoons apart; it should form a continuous thread.

1 Sift the flours into a large mixing bowl. Add the yogurt, yeast, and enough water to produce a thick batter of pouring consistency.

2 Put the water and sugar into a saucepan. Heat gently, stirring, until the sugar has dissolved. Bring to a boil and cook, still stirring, until the syrup has reached the thread stage, 225°F. Add the saffron and cardamom just before the syrup is ready. Set aside.

3 Heat the oil until a cube of day-old bread browns in 1 minute. Stir the batter again, and pour into the pan through a slotted spoon so that it forms long coils. Deep-fry a few coils at a time for 30 seconds, or until crisp and golden brown.

4 Drain the coils on paper towels and soak in the syrup for a few minutes until they are literally dripping with syrup. Serve immediately.

**VARIATION**

- Use a few drops of rose flower water in the batter mixture.
- Use ghee instead of oil.

# Rice Pudding

INDIANS BELIEVE *milk to be divine, which is perhaps why milk puddings are the perfect antidote to hot spicy foods.*

**INGREDIENTS**

*scant ½ cup basmati rice, soaked for 30 minutes, drained*

*7½ cups full-fat milk*

*1 teaspoon ground cardamom*

*scant ½ cup superfine sugar*

*2 heaping tablespoons shredded coconut*

*3 tablespoons golden raisins*

*3 tablespoons slivered almonds*

1 Bring the rice and half the milk to a boil in a large saucepan. Lower the heat and simmer gently for 30 minutes, stirring frequently. Add the remaining milk and cardamom.

2 Simmer, stirring frequently, for another 1–1¼ hours.

3 Add the sugar and coconut and cook for about 10–12 minutes. Cool slightly.

4 Pour into a shallow serving dish and decorate with golden raisins and almonds. Chill well before serving.

**COOK'S TIP**

If ground cardamom is not available, grind cardamom seeds.

# Further reading


INDIAN VEGETARIAN COOKING, *Louise Steele* (Parragon, 1994)

30 MINUTE INDIAN VEGETARIAN, *Mridular Baljekar* (Thorsons, 1997)

THE ART OF INDIAN VEGETARIAN COOKING, *Yamuna Devi* (Bala Books, 1987)

CLASSIC INDIAN VEGETARIAN COOKING, *Julie Sahni* (Grub Street, 1998)

"CURRY CLUB" INDIAN VEGETARIAN COOKBOOK, *Pat Chapman* (Piatkus Books, 1997)

INDIAN CUISINE: VEGETARIAN, (Tiger Books, 1996)

FLAVORS OF INDIA: VEGETARIAN INDIAN CUISINE, *Shanta Nimbark Sacharoff* (Book Publishing Company, 1996)

THE INDIAN VEGETARIAN, *Neelam Batra, Shelly Rothschild-Sherwin*, (Macmillan, 1994)

INDIAN VEGETARIAN COOKING, *Sumana Ray* (Apple Press, 1994)

INDIA: THE VEGETARIAN TABLE, *Yamuna Devi, Zeva Oelbaum* (Chronicle Books, 1997)

QUICK AND EASY INDIAN VEGETARIAN, *Veena Chopra* (Foulsham, 1995)


# Useful addresses

**The Vegetarian Society**
Parkdale
Durham Road
Altrincham
Cheshire WA14 4QG
UK

**The Vegetarian Union of North America**
PO Box 9710
Washington DC 20016
USA

**The Australian Vegetarian Society**
PO Box 65
2021 Paddington
Australia

**The Soil Association**
86 Colston Street
Bristol BS1 5BB
UK

**Farm Verified Organic**
RR 1
Box 40A USA
Medina
ND 58467
USA

**National Association for Sustainable Agriculture**
PO Box 768
AUS-Sterling
SA 5152
Australia

*Other Books in the Series*

SEASONAL EATING
A Step-by-Step Guide

EATING VEGETARIAN
A Step-by-Step Guide

HEALING FOODS
A Step-by-Step Guide

FOOD COMBINING
A Step-by-Step Guide

ITALIAN VEGETARIAN COOKING
A Step-by-Step Guide

FRENCH VEGETARIAN COOKING
A Step-by-Step Guide

THAI VEGETARIAN COOKING
A Step-by-Step Guide